STICKS, SPOOLS and FEATHERS

By Harvey Weiss

YOUNG SCOTT BOOKS

Table of Contents

Thanks and acknowledgements are due the following organizations and individuals for their cooperation and generous help in the preperation of this book: The Metropolitan Museum of Art, New York; The Museum of Modern Art, New York; The New York Central Railroad System; Mr. Buckminster Fuller; David Lasker; Carla Stevens.

The illustration at the top of page 3 is by David Lasker. Other illustrations and models are by the author unless otherwise credited.

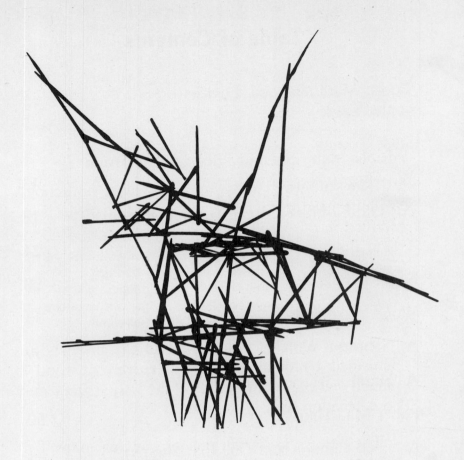

Introduction

The techniques and methods explained in this book can be used for many things besides the projects described. The information contained here can be combined with your own ideas and knowledge and experience, and applied in many ways.

For example, on page 34, there are directions for making a giraffe out of small pieces of wood. But suppose you would rather make a fat hippopotamus, or a fancy, polka-dotted ostrich, or a zebracrocodile with feathers? If you understand the instructions for making a giraffe, you can use these techniques to make any animal your fancy dictates.

Techniques and skills are tools—just as this book is a tool—and there is no limit to their use, because there is no limit to the imagination.

Tools, Materials and Tricks of the Trade

The following tools, found in most households, will be needed to make many of the projects described in this book:

hammer	chisels	screwdriver
saw	scissors	hacksaw
file	drill	plane
knife	counterpunch	sharpening stone
vise	pliers	scroll saw

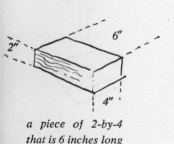

a piece of 2-by-4 that is 6 inches long

Various sizes of wood used in the projects are described by their dimensions. However, wood is planed smooth at the mill, so the actual sizes may be a fraction less.

The best wood for our purposes is clear pine. This is neither too hard nor too soft, and it can be worked easily. But you can get just about the same results from old crate or fruitbox lumber. You will simply have to spend more time in sandpapering or planing and filing to remove the rough surfaces. If you buy lumber at a lumberyard, avoid split wood and wood with knotholes.

NAILING: A good job of nailing depends on the choice of the nail. Too big a nail will split a thin piece of wood. Too small a nail won't hold. The kind of work described in this book is best done with brads. These nails are quite thin and have very small heads. If they are "punched" below the surface of the wood with a counterpunch, the remaining holes can be filled with plastic wood and then sanded smooth. Nails hold best when driven in at an angle, rather than straight down.

USING SCREWS: When joining two pieces of wood by means of a screw, be sure to drill a hole where the screw is to go. If you don't, the wood will probably split. The hole should be slightly smaller than the screw itself.

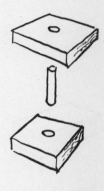

USING DOWELS: Dowels are also used to join two pieces of wood. Drill a hole, exactly the size of the dowel, through the two pieces of wood to be joined. Coat the dowel and the walls of the holes with glue; insert the dowel in the holes. Then weight or clamp the two pieces together for at least half an hour. You will have an extremely strong joint.

GLUING: There are many glues suitable for the work described in this book. Any fast-drying casein glue is good. Among the best is Elmer's Glue-All, which comes in a plastic bottle. For stick constructions of the type described in the first section of this book, a cement such as Duco is best. In gluing, it is important to clamp or weight the pieces of wood together while the glue dries.

SANDPAPERING: Sandpaper comes in several grades. Use a coarse grade for rough work and do your finishing with a fine grade. Wrap the sandpaper around a small block of wood so that you can hold it well to do a neat job.

PAINTING: Before painting wood, "seal" it with a thin coat of shellac or varnish. Rub this coat with fine sandpaper or steel wool before applying your colors. To paint a straight edge, use masking tape or adhesive tape placed at what is to be the edge of your color. Paint slightly onto the tape, then remove it. The tape acts as a ruler, and you get a neat, straight edge.

5

SKYBREAK DWELLING
designed by
Buckminster Fuller

Stick Towers

When you make this project, you must be half artist and half mechanical engineer. On the one hand, a stick tower is a *design of lines*. Each stick is a little straight line; added to other sticks, it makes a pattern or "drawing" that can be very handsome as a design.

And on the other hand, a stick tower is an *engineered construction*. It has to be planned so that it will hold together and keep its balance.

Constructions of this sort are used by many modern architects. They have found it economical to construct huge roofs in this way—without having to use a great many supporting columns and beams. The placement of the rods in this kind of structure is planned so that the weight of the roof spreads out evenly over a large area. Of course, instead of wooden sticks, they use heavy steel or aluminum rods covered over with a waterproof material. Buckminster Fuller, who designed the structure illustrated at the top of this page, pioneered this type of construction.

How To Make A Stick Tower

MATERIALS: This stick tower is made with toothpicks held together by a strong, fast-drying cement such as Duco Cement. One tube of cement and a box of toothpicks supply enough material for even the most ambitious construction. Get flat toothpicks rather than the round kind—they are a little easier to work with. (Actually, any small, thin sticks, such as lollipop sticks, split bamboo, or even uncooked spaghetti, can be used to make these structures.) You'll also need two or three spring-type clothespins.

1. Start your tower by cementing three toothpicks together to make a triangle. A small dab of cement on the tip of each toothpick is enough to make a strong joint.

2. This is a beginning. You can now proceed to add more toothpicks to your original triangle. Let this first part of your tower lie flat on its side to dry. You can stand it upright later.

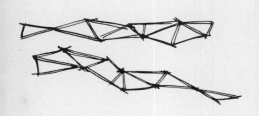

3. Cement takes five or ten minutes to dry, so begin another section of your tower while the first part is drying. The trick, in putting a tower like this together, is to make as many separate parts as possible on a flat surface. *Then,* when the cement is dry, combine the sections to form a larger structure. If you tried to build your tower upright, stick by stick, you would spend most of the time holding the sticks in place while the cement hardened.

4. When you have two or more sections of the tower completed, join them by applying cement where they meet. Then clamp them together with a clothespin until the cement dries.

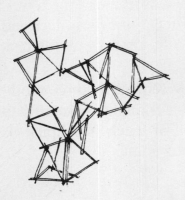

5. You can keep building a tower like this—a section at a time—for as long as you have cement, toothpicks, and patience. However, don't get so involved in the mechanics of making a sturdy structure that you forget all about creating something handsome to look at.

9

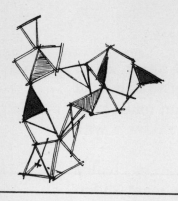

6. You can brighten up your tower by fitting pieces of colored paper into some of the open spaces. Cut the paper exactly to the shape of the space you are about to fill. Then use a dab of cement on the corners to hold it in place.

7. If your tower has a small base and seems a little wobbly or tipsy, cement it to a wooden block which will serve as a base. Or, why not try suspending your tower by a thread from the ceiling? It will look especially nice if there is a lamp near by which throws a shadow of your tower onto the wall or ceiling.

Dowel Towers

Large, exciting constructions can be made with wooden dowels and wire, instead of toothpicks and cement. Dowels are thin rods of wood, three feet long, which can be obtained at a lumberyard or a hardware store. Fifty or more ¼-inch dowels will make a tremendous tower, one that can reach as high as fifteen or twenty feet and can spread out over a large area in almost any interesting shape.

Dowels are too heavy to be cemented together. Join them by wrapping wire around the ends. Use a very thin, galvanized iron wire and tighten securely by twisting the ends of the wire with a pair of pliers.

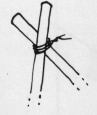

THE RAPE OF LUCRECE, by Reuben Nakian. This statue is made of painted steel and stands almost twelve feet high. Photograph courtesy of the Museum of Modern Art. ▶

The dowels can be used over and over again. After you've made a tower or two, you may want to construct a little house by this same method. You can make your house snug and waterproof by covering the dowels with a sheet of thin plastic.

In fact, an infinite variety of structures can be created with this technique. You can explore it in many different directions. For example, you might want to attempt some kind of perfectly balanced mechanical construction such as a bridge, an oil drilling tower, or a radar antenna—using either toothpicks and cement or dowels and wires.

Or, you may prefer a construction that is simply fun to look at. A number of modern sculptors work in a fashion similar to this. They make open, airy statues that contain no solid forms at all—only rods and sticks and thin plates of steel and sometimes wires, combined to make an interesting and dramatic design.

Weaving

Weaving is a technique that goes back as far as recorded history itself. The piece of fabric illustrated at the top of this page, for example, was made by a Peruvian weaver hundreds of years ago. It was woven on a primitive loom. To the left of that is a strip of Mexican material similar to the kind made many centuries ago.

Weaving is simply the interlacing of threads over and under one another. Any kind of yarn or string or thread can be woven. You can even weave your fingers, as the photograph in the margin indicates.

Most of the cloth you wear is woven from threads of cotton or wool or rayon or nylon combined in

any number of different patterns and colors. But the basic principle of weaving is the same for a fancy velvet drape, a delicate silk scarf, or a piece of rough burlap.

The looms that weave commercial cloth today are huge, intricate, power-driven machines. But you can make a simple loom on which to weave a tie, or a belt, or a place mat, with just a handful of nails and a few pieces of board. This will give you some understanding of the principles of weaving. And, with a little practice, you can use your loom to make a tie or a place mat as handsome as any to be found in the fanciest shops. The fabrics illustrated at the top of this page and on page 17 were all made on the type of loom described in this section.

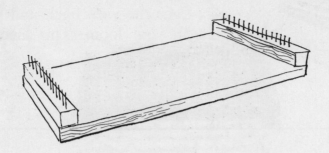

The Loom

MATERIALS: You will need a piece of board approximately 6 inches wide and 18 inches long, two strips of wood about 1 inch by 1 inch and 6 inches long, and thirty 1½-inch nails.

TOOLS: Hammer, drill, coarse-toothed comb, and scissors.

The loom, as assembled, is shown in the diagram above. Nail the two strips of wood to the board, then—in pencil—mark the places where the projecting nails are to go. These nails should be placed in a straight line, one quarter of an inch apart. Hammer the nails about halfway into the wood strips, and your loom is ready to be used.

Weaving a Place Mat

1. Get some wool or cotton yarn. Knitting yarn is most suitable, but you can use string or twine if nothing else is handy. (Sewing thread, or any very thin yarn, would break too easily and is too delicate to handle.)

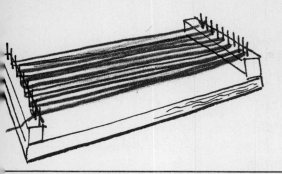

2. Lace the yarn back and forth around the nails in your loom. This laced yarn is called the *warp*.

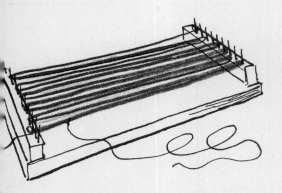

3. Now you can start to weave. Take a piece of yarn about three feet long and tie the end of it to the outside warp, as illustrated. This yarn can be a different color and weight from the warp.

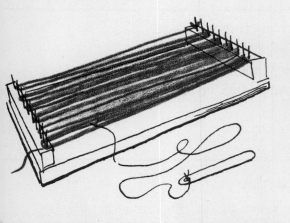

4. Get a tongue depressor or a popsicle stick, drill a hole in one end, thread the free end of the yarn through this hole, and tie it. This stick is called the *shuttle;* it acts as a sort of sewing needle.

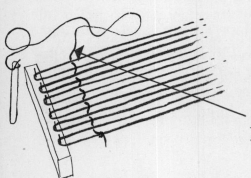

5. Lace the shuttle over and under the warp, and then pull the yarn through.

Don't pull yarn too tight or your fabric will become very narrow.

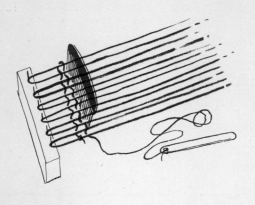

6. Repeat the process, going back in the opposite direction. After each such pass, use a coarse-toothed comb to push the yarn up against the previous strand so that it is close and tight. This "combing" is an important part of the weaving process and should be done neatly and carefully.

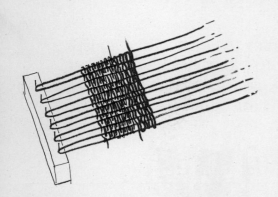

7. When you've used up your first length of yarn, take another piece and continue. It is not necessary to knot one piece of yarn to another. Let the end of the first piece hang loose, and just continue with the next length. When your work is completed, you can snip off the protruding ends with a pair of scissors.

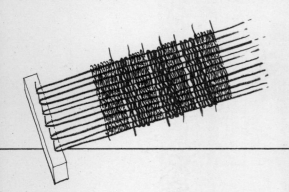

8. If you use a different color for each successive length of yarn, your place mat will have a series of stripes.

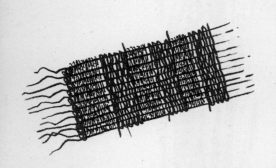

9. Complete your place mat by cutting the warp off the nails, one strand at a time, and knotting it to the next, adjoining strand. This prevents unraveling. Another way to finish off a piece of fabric is by stitching the ends, either by hand or by sewing machine. If your place mat looks a bit small, make another and sew the two together. To make a large piece of fabric—a scarf, or a wall hanging, for example— you will have to weave many small sections and sew them together.

The design of a tree is sewn, or "embroidered" onto the finished fabric.

Even though this is the very simplest type of loom, you can produce very handsome fabrics by working carefully and using an attractive combination of colors. Try to choose varied colors that do not contrast too violently. Experiment with different weights and thicknesses of yarn.

You can add color and texture to your fabric by knotting short lengths of yarn onto the warp. The little tufts will stick out through the woven fabric. Or, simply lace into the warp one-inch or two-inch pieces of contrastingly colored yarn.

One advantage of working with a small, basic loom—like the one described here—is that it makes experimenting easy. If you don't like the way a new idea is turning out, it is a simple matter to unravel and start again.

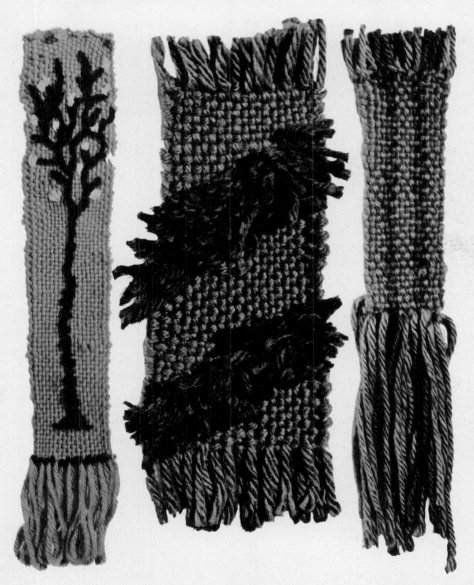

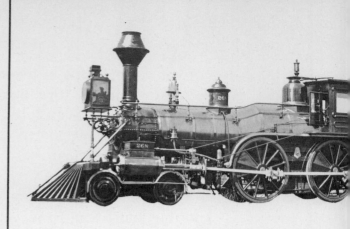

An Old-Fashioned Steam Locomotive

Until a few years ago steam locomotives—like those shown above—were the only kind used on American railroads. They were beautiful, noisy machines that hissed and shuddered and blew out enormous clouds of steam and smoke and cinders. They were painted and polished with loving care. They had gleaming brass valve mechanisms, a whistle, and a huge bronze bell.

Of course, steam locomotives came in many shapes and forms, depending on their use. Some had only four wheels, others had as many as ten or twelve. And there were all kinds of different domes and smokestacks and cabs and cow-catchers.

A model of one of these picturesque old steam engines is nice to have and fun to make. It can be constructed of the simplest materials. Make your model to suit your *own* idea of how a steam locomotive should look. Try to capture the spirit and excitement and good looks of these elegant old machines, rather than an exact mechanical likeness.

How to Make an Old-Fashioned Steam Locomotive

MATERIALS: You will need 1 foot of ½-inch by 2-inch clear pine, a short piece of 1-inch by 3-inch clear pine, a piece of broomstick or 1-inch dowel, some thread spools, a foot of ¼-inch dowel, 6 inches of ¾-inch dowel, a fast-drying glue (such as Elmer's Glue-All or Duco Cement), sandpaper, paint, and some brass or iron wire. (Be sure to read the section on Tools, Materials, and Tricks of the Trade at the beginning of this book before starting to build your locomotive.)

TOOLS: File, drill, screwdriver, and saw.

1. Cut off a length of broomstick for the boiler. File or plane the bottom slightly flat, then sandpaper thoroughly. All parts of this engine should be sandpapered carefully before they are put together.

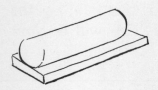

2. Cut off a piece of the ½-inch by 2-inch pine. Make it about an inch longer than the boiler. Drill holes for screws, then glue and screw this piece to the bottom of your boiler.

NOTE: If you can't obtain all the materials mentioned in these directions, try to find substitutes—combine various materials that you do have, to approximate what you need. (Or, change the design of your locomotive to suit the materials you *do* have.)

Suppose, for example, you can't get a dowel for the smokestack of your engine. You may have a square piece of wood that can be filed or planed or whittled until round —or use a spool, a piece of curtain rod, or a cardboard tube—or make a square smokestack! These instructions are intended to show you *one* way of working. You may prefer to use your own ideas.

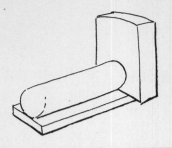

3. Make the cab from the 1-inch by 3-inch pine. File it slightly round on top and fasten as indicated.

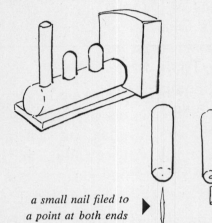

4. Make the smokestack from a piece of ¾-inch dowel. Drill a ¾-inch hole in the top of the boiler and glue the smokestack into it. You can make the domes in the same way, or you can use half of a thread spool for each. Two alternate ways of attaching the smokestack and domes to the boiler are shown.

a small nail filed to a point at both ends ▶

◀ *a small dowel set into a hole in base of smokestack and glued into another hole in boiler.*

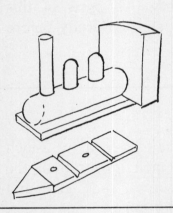

5. Cut a length of wood from your ½-inch by 2-inch pine for the bottom of the locomotive. File two grooves, into which your axles will fit. Drill two holes for screws. Saw the wood to a point at one end. This will be your cow-catcher.

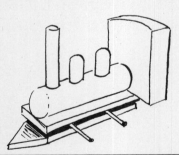

6. Cut the axles from ¼-inch dowel. They should be 4 inches long. They are held in place when the bottom strip, with the two grooves, is screwed on tightly.

7. The wheels are made from narrow slices sawed from a broomstick or spool. Drill a ¼-inch hole in the center of each wheel.

21

8. Drill thin holes in the axles, as illustrated. A wooden peg, or a loop of wire, passed through these little holes will keep the wheels from coming off. If you don't have a small enough drill, saw a notch in the end of the axles and glue in a thin strip of wood.

9. Now add the accessories—lights and bells and whistle. Most of these things can be whittled out of wood and simply glued on. Then you can drill holes into which wire railing and piping will fit. Any self-respecting steam locomotive has yards and yards of pipes and rails.

10. Finally, give your engine a coat of shellac or varnish. Then paint it. Use a lacquer or enamel—the brighter, the better.

After you have made the locomotive, you'll find it easy to make the tender and freight or passenger cars.

The illustrations on the page opposite show some other things that can be made with the same techniques you used for the locomotive. And you can probably think of a great many other possibilities yourself.

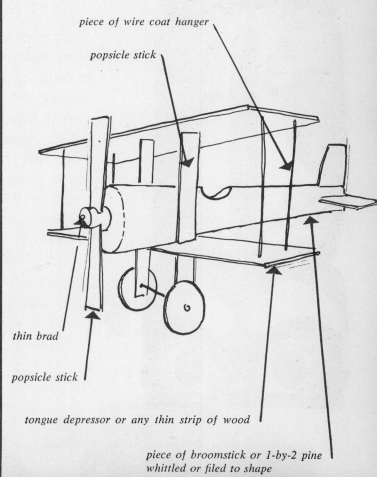

piece of wire coat hanger

popsicle stick

thin brad

popsicle stick

tongue depressor or any thin strip of wood

piece of broomstick or 1-by-2 pine whittled or filed to shape

Totem Poles

The Indians of the Northwest live in an area where there are many forests. So it is to be expected that wood is an important part of their culture. They live in houses of wood, they use canoes made of hollowed-out cedar logs, and many of their everyday utensils are wooden. But their most dramatic use of wood is the totem pole—a huge log, sometimes as tall as a three- or four-story building, carved with fanciful heads and animals and birds, and painted in vivid colors. The Indians carved totem poles to guard against evil spirits and to commemorate events of importance.

You can carve your own totem pole from a piece of wood. (It doesn't have to be seventy feet high.) Make a little base and stand it on a table or bookshelf. Besides looking very attractive, it may guard *you* against evil spirits.

Detail of a totem pole made by John and Fred Wallace.
The complete pole stands thirty-two feet high. Photograph
courtesy of the Museum of Modern Art, New York.

How to Make a Totem Pole

MATERIALS: You will need a log about as thick as your arm and about 2 feet long. If you can't find a suitable log, use a piece of 4-inch by 4-inch pine; cut off the corners until it becomes more or less round. You'll also need sandpaper, some plastic wood, and paint.

TOOLS: Knife, chisel, gouges, vise, drill, file, hammer, and sharpening stone.

1. Make a few rough drawings on paper before you start. You can refer to these as you carve your wood. Make your totem pole as fanciful as you wish, with strange animals or birds and grotesque faces. You'll rarely find anything very realistic-looking on a totem pole.

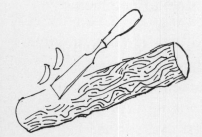

2. If you are working with a log, first whittle or chisel off all the bark.

3. Now, with a soft pencil, indicate roughly on the log where each element of your design is to go. Remember that the actual carving of your totem pole can be quite simple and undetailed, because small things such as eyes and teeth and nostrils can be painted rather than carved.

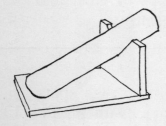

4. Put your log in a vise, or clamp it to your work table to hold it in place while you are working. You'll have trouble carving if it keeps slipping and turning about. If you don't have a vise or a clamp, make a holder like the one illustrated.

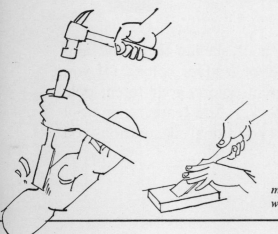

5. Begin by carving away the wood from your main forms with a large chisel. Remember that in carving, what you *don't* touch will stand out. Keep your chisels as sharp as possible by rubbing them often on your sharpening stone, as illustrated.

move the chisel back and forth with a steady even motion

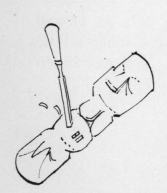

6. When you have carved away the wood from your main forms, shift to a smaller chisel or gouge or a whittling knife and work on some of the smaller forms.

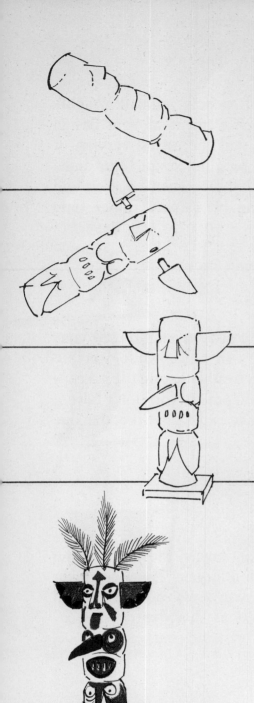

7. Keep turning your log, so that you can work on the sides and back as well as the front. You want the totem pole to look good from all sides.

8. Parts such as noses, ears, wings, and horns can be carved out of separate pieces of wood and then fitted into holes drilled in the log. Fit them carefully, use a few drops of glue, and they will stay in place permanently.

9. Now file and sandpaper any rough spots and repair little splits and cracks with plastic wood. Cut out a square piece of wood for a base; nail or screw this base to the log.

10. Finally, varnish or shellac the wood and paint it with enamel or lacquer colors. (If you use too many different colors, your totem pole will have a gaudy look.) Add feathers, or wool yarn, or whatever additional decoration you think necessary.

If you want to mount your totem pole on a wall (which will give it quite a dramatic look), make a little bracket like the one illustrated below. You can fasten this bracket to your wall with just one nail.

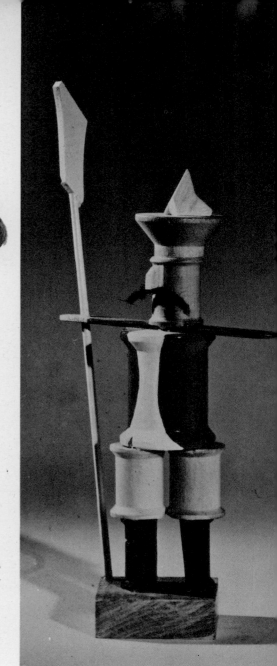

Spool People

Have you ever looked at an empty thread spool and wondered what you could do with it? Well, the characters above show one good use for empty spools. These colorful little figures are made of a handful of spools, with just a few little odds and ends added for decoration.

Your work is made easy in a figure of this sort, because the shape of a spool is so suggestive—it resembles so many different things. A spool can be a hat, a head, a trouser leg, and many other things. So you are off to a good start. When you make something—in sculpture or drawing or painting or in any medium—and you use shapes that are interesting and well proportioned, the combination of these shapes will probably also look pleasing.

A Spoolman Pirate

MATERIALS: Find as many spools of different sizes and shapes as you can. You will also need some popsicle sticks or tongue depressors, a strong and fast-drying glue (such as Elmer's Glue-All or Duco Cement), sandpaper, and some bright enamel colors.

TOOLS: Hacksaw, file, and whittling knife.

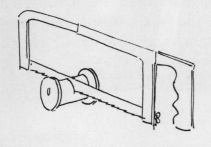

1. File or sandpaper the paper labels off the ends of each spool; then sandpaper the entire spool until it is clean and smooth.

2. Cut a small spool in half for the head. (A hacksaw works best on spools.)

3. If you want your pirate to look fierce, you must certainly give him a fierce-looking nose! Whittle a little piece of wood for the nose and glue it in place.

4. Use a larger spool for the body. Cut two slits in the rim of this spool. Whittle a tongue depressor or a popsicle stick to the shape of an arm. Glue the arms into the slots.

5. Now glue the head to the body.

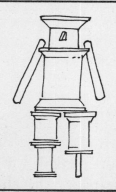

6. Assemble some smaller spools for the legs. If you don't have small spools, take a single large one, cut it in half lengthwise, and glue the two halves to the body.

This pirate has a "peg-leg" which is made of a short length of dowel.

7. Paint your spoolman carefully, using a fine brush. Finally, add the little extras—the feather in the hat, the wool beard and mustache, the ribbon belt, and the popsicle-stick sword.

The appearance of a spool figure depends largely on your imagination and ingenuity in devising little accessories such as hair, hat, skirt, and so on. The care and thought you give to the final painting are also very important.

You can make a *miniature* totem pole (like the one described in the preceding section), without having to do any carving, from five or six spools. The drawing to the right shows how this can be done.

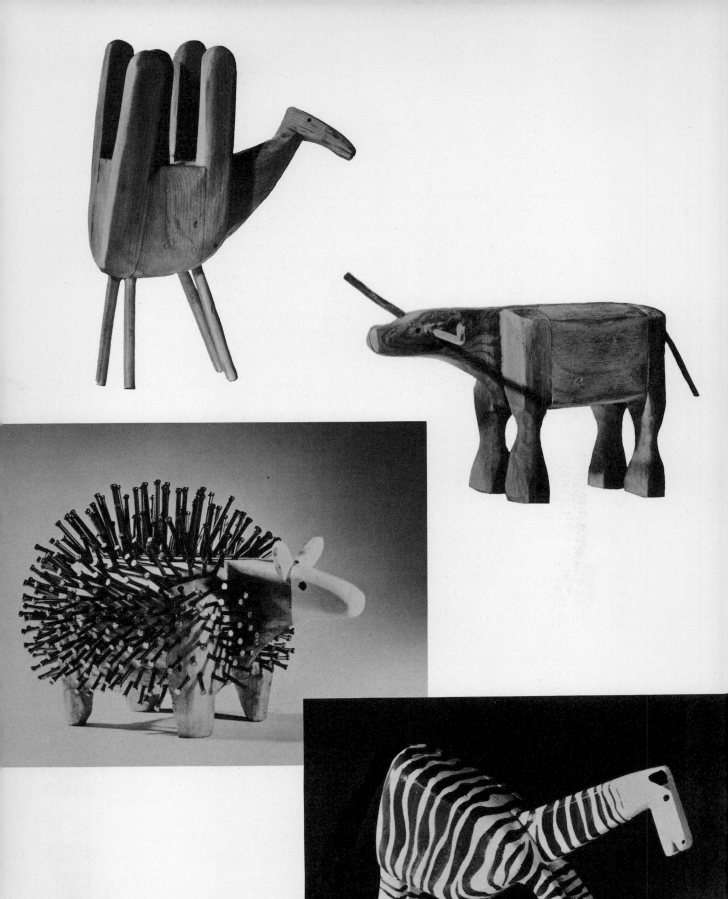

Wooden Animals

Carving is the conventional way to make a wooden animal or figure. That is how you made the totem pole described in an earlier section of this book. You carved all the unwanted wood away from a large block, leaving only the shapes of your subject.

But there is another way to make wooden animals— by *building up,* using separate, small pieces of wood glued and nailed together.

There are two advantages to the latter method. First, working in this fashion allows you to get long, thin (or flat) shapes that would probably splinter or break off if you carved them out of one piece of wood. Second, you save time and tedious work by not having to carve away the wood you don't want.

The illustrations on the page opposite will give you an idea of the kinds of things you can make in this "building-up" fashion. The steer is constructed with only seven pieces of wood. Notice how nicely the grain of the wood shows up in this little animal. Each individual piece of wood has its own grain, so that when the completed work has been sanded smooth and shellacked, the differing grains make a very attractive pattern.

The other unlikely-looking animals illustrated are not to be found in any zoo on this earth. For some reason, the *building-up* method has a tendency to produce strange and humorous creatures...like that camel with five humps!

How to Make a Giraffe

MATERIALS: You will need a 3-foot strip of ½-inch by 2-inch clear pine, 3 feet of ½-inch by ½-inch pine, thin headless nails (called brads), a fast-drying casein glue (such as Elmer's Glue-All), some plastic wood, medium- and fine-grade sandpaper, and shellac. (Before starting this project, read the section Tools, Materials, and Tricks of the Trade, at the beginning of this book.)

TOOLS: Saw, file, hammer, and counterpunch.

1. Cut off a 1½-inch piece of the ½-inch by ½-inch pine; file it into the shape of a giraffe's head. Use the sharp edge of your file to make a groove for the mouth, then round off the top for the nose. Make little nail holes for eyes.

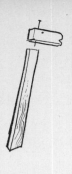

2. Cut off an 8-inch piece of the ½-inch by ½-inch pine for the neck. Glue and nail the head to it. Use a very thin nail to avoid splitting the wood.

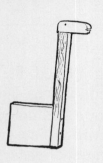

3. The body is made of five pieces of the ½-inch by 2-inch pine. Cut out the center piece first. It should be about 3 inches long. Nail and glue the neck to the edge of this center piece. (If you want the giraffe's neck to be leaning forward, make a cut at an angle where it joins the body.)

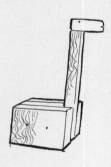

4. Cut two more pieces for the body. Make sure that each equals the combined length of the body center piece plus the neck. Glue and nail one piece to each side of the center one.

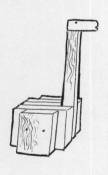

5. Now cut two more pieces for the body. Each of these should be an inch shorter than the rest of the body, so that there will be room for legs at either end. Glue and nail these in place.

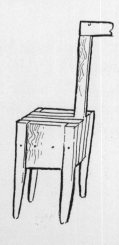

6. The legs are made from ½-inch by ½-inch pine, filed round. Glue and nail these in place.

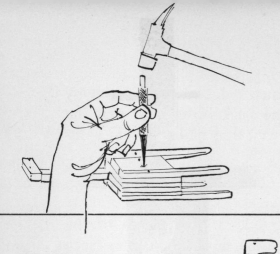

7. Now take a counterpunch, or another nail, and drive all nailheads below the surface of the wood. Fill the nail holes, and any gaps or splits, with plastic wood.

8. When the plastic wood has dried, file and sandpaper the entire giraffe until it is as smooth as possible. Start with a rough or medium grade of sandpaper and finish off with a fine grade. Take your time with this operation, because the final appearance of your giraffe depends on how you do the finishing.

9. Nail two short brads, for the horns, onto the head. Apply a coat of shellac or varnish to the giraffe. Let the shellac or varnish dry. Then polish it with fine sandpaper or steel wool, and consider it finished. If you can still see rough spots and a good deal of patching, give the giraffe a bright coat of paint.

These instructions tell you how to make a giraffe, but you can use this method to construct anything from a hippopotamus to an alligator or a human figure—by merely changing the size and number and proportion and placement of the parts. The illustrations on the page opposite suggest some other possibilities, and no doubt you have many ideas of your own. The photograph on the lower right hand side of the page shows still another way of using this same "building-up" technique. This rather elaborate-looking abstract sculpture is simply made of many variously sized pieces of wood glued together (but without nails) in the same manner as your giraffe.

This is a Chagu-Chagu
or Japanese "Horse of the Gods." ▶

A Tightrope Walker

There is a mechanical principle stating that a small *heavy* object will balance a large but *lighter* object. Try this little experiment to see how the principle actually works. Straighten out a paper clip and bend a small loop near one end. Fasten a little ball of clay to the short end, and a feather or a piece of paper to the other end. Then run another straightened-out paper clip through the loop. The small clay ball—because it is relatively heavy—will keep the large light feather or paper balancing up in the air.

This simple fact has many interesting applications, some of which are illustrated on the page opposite. The tightrope walker, for example, does not fall off his precarious perch because the two small objects which hang down below the rope are relatively heavy steel nuts, and the tightrope walker himself is made of light cardboard. The same principle keeps those balsa wood acrobats balancing.

If you run a thread from one side of your room to the other, you can have one of these fellows balancing up in the air in the gayest fashion. Or, make several—have a whole circus troop performing for you!

How to Make a Tightrope Walker

MATERIALS: You will need a thin slab of balsa wood or a piece of cardboard (the kind that comes with a laundered shirt), some small heavy weights (such as the lead sinkers that fishermen use or a few steel nuts and bolts), adhesive tape, and a few feet of galvanized iron wire. The wire should be about as thick as this line ————

TOOLS: Sharp knife or scroll saw for balsa wood, or scissors for cardboard.

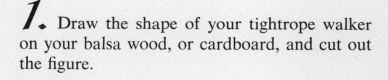

1. Draw the shape of your tightrope walker on your balsa wood, or cardboard, and cut out the figure.

2. Bend the wire to the shape indicated and fasten it to the back of the figure with thin strips of adhesive tape.

3. Now attach the weights to the ends of the wire. Stretch a string or a thread between two points in your room and try out your tightrope walker. If he balances a little lopsidedly, adjust the weights and wire.

4. Finally, you can sandpaper and paint him.

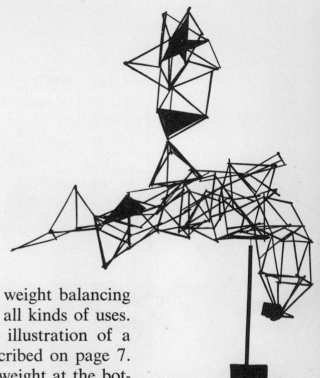

The principle of a small *heavy* weight balancing a large *light* weight can be put to all kinds of uses. For example, on the right is an illustration of a large stick tower like the one described on page 7. It is balanced by the small heavy weight at the bottom of the tower, and the whole thing will sway and spin merrily on a single balancing point. If placed in a draft, it will move about continually.

A small wheel with a groove around its edge is all you need to make a unicyclist. The drawing below shows how this brave fellow is put together.

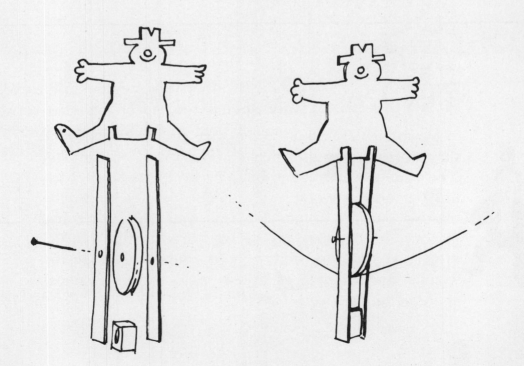

41

A Simple Electric Motor that Works

Most machines in use today give you no hint of how they operate, because their working parts are hidden. You cannot watch a gasoline engine operating and figure out how it works; all you can usually see is the motor's outside casing. Nor can you see an electric motor working; the only visible parts are the outside protective covering and a protruding shaft. All the wonder and excitement of electrical and mechanical action is hidden.

This is not true of the little electric motor described in this section. You can see all the parts of this motor in operation. It will spin around at a great rate, humming and sparking, and you can watch it and understand exactly how it works.

A simple, neat, efficient little piece of machinery appears as beautiful to some people as a Rembrandt painting does to others. When this little motor starts buzzing away, you will probably find it handsome indeed.

This motor will also demonstrate quite clearly some basic electrical principles. All electric motors are based on one fact—an electric current flowing through a wire

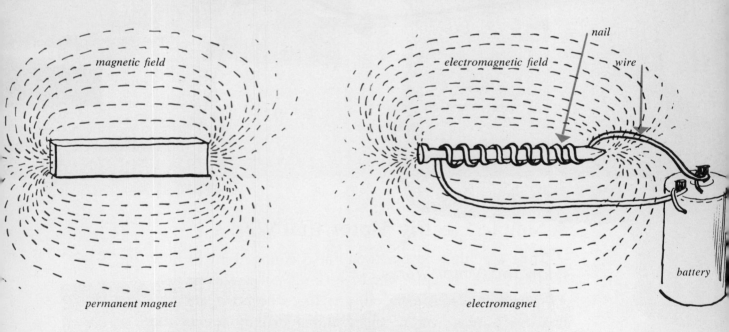

magnetic field

permanent magnet

electromagnetic field

nail

wire

battery

electromagnet

will set up an electromagnetic field. This field, like a magnet's field, will attract steel or iron. When a wire is wrapped around a nail, as in our motor, and an electric current flows through this wire, the nail becomes an electromagnet.

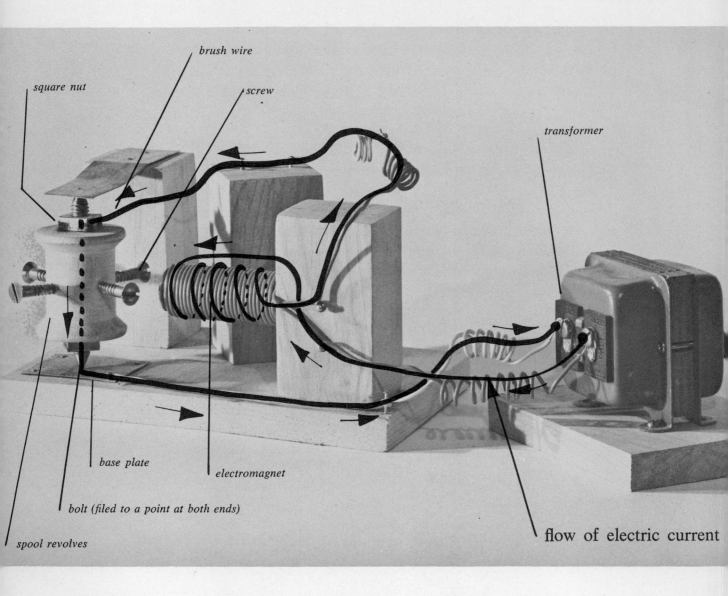

brush wire

square nut

screw

transformer

base plate

electromagnet

bolt (filed to a point at both ends)

spool revolves

flow of electric current

How this Motor Works

The flow of electric current in our motor is as follows: it comes from the transformer or battery and goes through the electromagnet. From here it goes through the brush wire to the rotating nut, and from the nut down through the bolt—which is in the center of the spool—to the base plate. From there it goes back to the transformer or battery, completing the circuit.

The action of the motor is like this: the current comes out of the battery or transformer and goes through the wire which is wrapped around the nail, creating an electromagnetic field. This field (or magnet) attracts the

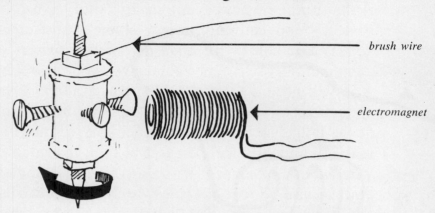

brush wire

electromagnet

screw on the spool. It pulls the screw and, in doing this, makes the spool rotate. As the spool rotates, the square nut on top of the spool also rotates. In rotating, the nut breaks contact with the brush wire. There is a gap. This interrupts the circuit. No current flows now. There is no

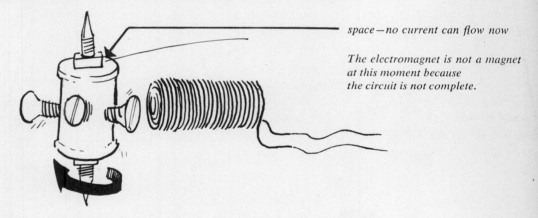

space—no current can flow now

The electromagnet is not a magnet at this moment because the circuit is not complete.

magnetism. But the spool continues to rotate because of the momentum it has been given. And as it rotates, the next corner of the nut makes contact with the brush wire. Once more current flows. The magnetic field is created again, and the next screw on the spool is attracted. And so on. In other words, the electromagnet is giving each screw on the spool a little tug at just the right moment, causing the spool to rotate.

How to Build this Motor

MATERIALS: The most important part of this motor is the source of power. An electric train transformer is perfect. You can also use a chime transformer (16 volts). You can even use an automobile battery or any combination of batteries that gives you 9 to 12 volts. You will need a large thread spool, a 3-inch bolt large enough to fit snugly inside the spool, and two nuts to fit the bolt. For the electromagnet you will need a large nail and approximately 50 feet of thin, insulated copper wire (about 30 gauge). If you can't get this kind of wire, you can use 25 feet of "bell wire," which is available in any hardware store. You will also need four large, flat-headed screws, a few blocks of wood, some strips of tin or copper, glue, and some thumbtacks.

TOOLS: Vise, drill, hacksaw, file, screwdriver, and hammer.

1. As exactly as possible, mark on your spool the position for the four large screws. They should be exactly opposite one another. Drill narrow holes into the spool and insert the screws.

2. Cut off the head of a large bolt with a hacksaw. The bolt should be about 1½ inches longer than your spool and it should be approximately the same diameter as the hole in the spool. File each end of this bolt to as fine and sharp a point as you can — needle sharp.

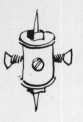

3. Put the bolt into the hole of the spool. If the bolt is a little loose, wrap some tape around it until it fits tightly. Screw on the nuts at top and bottom. Now you have the rotating part of your motor. It is called an "armature."

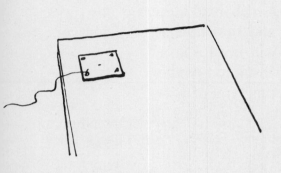

4. Cut a piece of wood about 4 inches by 8 inches for a base. Cut out a 1-inch by 1-inch piece of tin or copper and tack it near a corner of the base. Wrap the end of a short length of wire around one of the nails holding this little plate. Then make a *very slight* dent in the center of this plate with a nail or centerpunch.

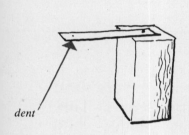

dent

5. Cut a block of wood about 2 inches by 4 inches and as tall as your armature. Take a strip of tin or copper about 1 inch wide and 3 inches long, and put a dent near one end of it. Tack this to the top of the block of wood. (The hollow part of the dent should be on the underneath side.)

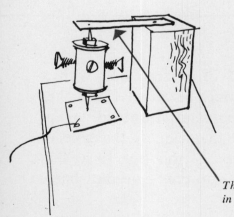

6. Now you can put your armature in place. Before you go any further, make any corrections or adjustments necessary in order to have the spool rotate freely and effortlessly. If you touch the spool lightly, it should revolve for quite a few turns with the minimum of friction.

This strip should just barely hold the spool in place and not press down too hard.

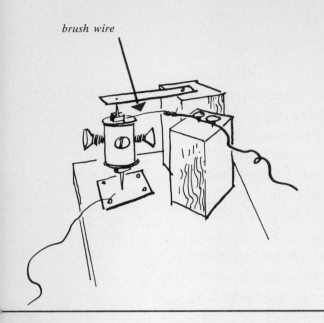

brush wire

7. Cut another block of wood slightly shorter than the armature. Fasten a piece of wire to the top with thumbtacks. Then wrap a short length of *very thin* copper wire around this, allowing it to project beyond the heavier wire by about an inch. This is your brush wire. (It *brushes* against the revolving nut.) The wire for this brush can be obtained from a piece of appliance wire. Cut off the insulation and unwrap a single strand of the thin copper wire for your brush.

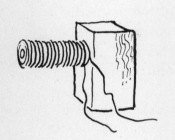

8. Next, you can make the electromagnet. Cut out a block of wood about 2 inches by 2 inches and 3 inches high. Drive a heavy nail into it at exactly the same height as the screws on your spool. Wrap the nail with your insulated copper wire—neatly—until you have built up about five or six layers of wire.

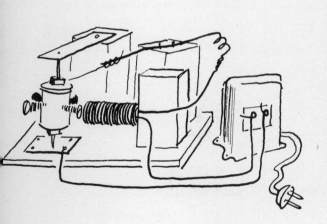

9. Connect all the wires as shown in the drawing. Adjust the brush wire so that it just barely touches the corners of the nut. Then position the electromagnet so that it is between two screws, and as close as possible to the screws without actually touching them as they revolve. Now plug in your transformer, or connect the batteries, give the armature a little twirl, and off you go!

The one extremely critical part of this motor is the brush wire. It has to touch with just the slightest pressure, and at just the right time. It should be just touching the corner of the nut when the electromagnet is at an equal distance between two screws. No doubt you will have to fuss patiently until you get this adjustment exactly right. When the adjustment is correct, you can glue the block of wood holding the electromagnet—and the block holding the brush wire—to the base.

This little motor can also be used as a radio transmitter! Run the motor and turn on a radio within a distance of a hundred feet or so; you will be able to hear a static sound—which is produced by the brush sparking against the revolving nut. Radio waves can be produced by a spark. In fact, the very first radio transmitters were spark transmitters. When your motor is working fast and efficiently, you can signal to a friend at a nearby radio by making a little key or switch to open and close the motor circuit. However, any neighbors who happen to be listening to their radios at the time will take a rather dim view of all this. This motor can also send a little white line flickering across a television screen.

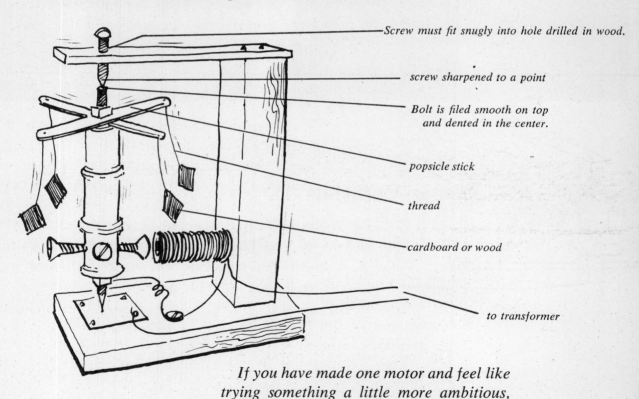

—Screw must fit snugly into hole drilled in wood.

screw sharpened to a point

Bolt is filed smooth on top and dented in the center.

popsicle stick

thread

cardboard or wood

to transformer

If you have made one motor and feel like trying something a little more ambitious, you might build the motor illustrated above. This is made with three spools and has four little arms with dangling weights. Note that the brush wire is placed at the bottom of the spools, touching the lower nut.

Paper Mad Hats

You can play many roles with the aid of paper hats.
Would you like to be a court jester, a colonel in the
Czar's cavalry, a man from outer space, a dragon, a
medieval knight, or a pirate captain? One of the hats
illustrated on the page opposite is realistic, one is fanciful, others—like the two at the top of this page—are a
little like paper sculpture (a sculpture to wear on your
head). The combination of forms and colors in each
hat is chosen to make as handsome a design as possible.
Paper hats are not only fun to wear, they are fun to
make!

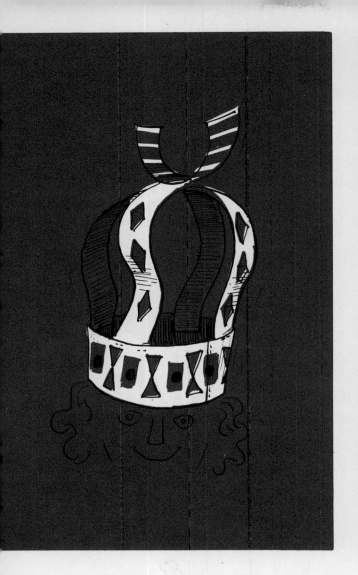

How to Make a Paper Hat

MATERIALS: You will need paints, newspapers, and string or tape. These hats can also be made of heavy brown wrapping paper or colored construction paper.

TOOLS: Scissors and stapler (or use glue instead of stapler).

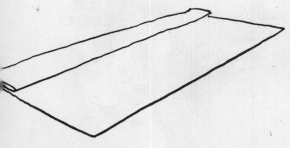

1. Take a double page of newspaper and fold it into a long, thin strip about 3 inches wide.

2. Wrap this strip around your head, just above the ears. Mark the place where the edge overlaps.

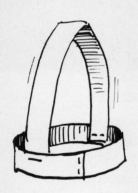

3. Staple or paste this edge in place. This band should fit snugly, but comfortably, on your head. It is the starting point and the basic part of any paper hat.

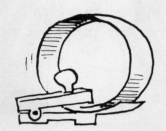

4. If you are making a hat like the one illustrated at the top of this page, your next step is to fold another strip of newspaper until it is about 4 inches wide. Staple or glue the ends of this strip to the headband, as illustrated.

5. Fold another, smaller, piece of paper into a square. Shred one end of the square and staple this to the top of the hat.

6. Now squeeze together the top part of the hat and wrap it with string or tape, so that it remains firm and upright.

7. Finish the hat by painting or decorating. See what effects you get by pasting on feathers, sequins, strips of gift-wrapping paper, or ribbons.

You have made a fairly simple kind of paper hat. Using the basic idea of the headband, you can design many other kinds of hats—your imagination can run wild!

Experiment with materials other than newspaper. Hats made with construction paper are usually very bright and lively because of the many possible color combinations. Leftover wallpaper will also prove useful, and cardboard and corrugated board come in handy. The stiffness of these last two materials enables you to make very large, spreadout hats—such as the one illustrated at the top of page 51.

A Naval Cannon

The type of cannon described here was used on most sailing ships during the eighteenth and nineteenth centuries. It had four small wheels because it only had to be moved short distances for aiming. It was loaded from the muzzle. First a charge of powder was rammed in. Then the cannon ball was shoved in on top of that. Finally, a light was placed at the breech hole and—BOOM—off it went.

The elevation of the barrel was controlled by a little wedge-shaped block of wood at the rear. If this block was thrust forward, the muzzle went down—pulled back, the muzzle went up.

A little cannon model makes a fine paperweight or book end.

How to Make this Cannon

MATERIALS: You will need a few pieces of 1-inch by 2-inch pine, a piece of ¼-inch dowel, a few strips of thin copper or tin (or aluminum foil), and a piece of broomstick or heavy dowel for the barrel, and sandpaper. If you can't get a length of broomstick or heavy dowel, glue three thread spools together for the barrel. (Remove the paper labels completely before you apply the glue.)

TOOLS: Saw, file, drill, and hammer.

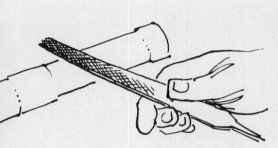

1. If you make the barrel out of a broomstick or heavy dowel, file it slowly and carefully to the shape you want. Keep turning the wood as you work, so that the contour remains even. If you are using spools, file down the rims at the center of the barrel.

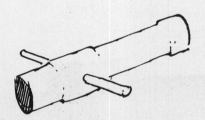

2. Drill a hole across the barrel and insert a dowel, as shown. Your drill should be the same size as the dowel (¼ inch), so that you get a snug fit.

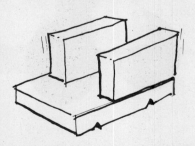

3. The gun carriage is made of 1-inch by 2-inch pine. Cut the pieces to the shape indicated, and fasten together with nails and glue. File two grooves in the bottom for the axles.

4. Cut two 5-inch pieces of ¼-inch dowel. These are your axles.

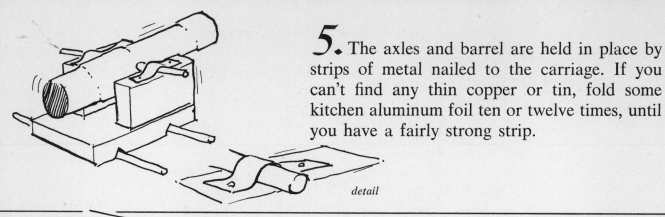

5. The axles and barrel are held in place by strips of metal nailed to the carriage. If you can't find any thin copper or tin, fold some kitchen aluminum foil ten or twelve times, until you have a fairly strong strip.

detail

6. Saw the wheels from a piece of broomstick, thick dowel, or a spool. Drill ¼-inch holes in the center.

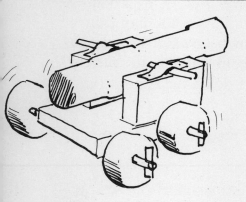

7. Mount the wheels on the axles. Keep each one from slipping off by sawing a groove in the end of the axle and gluing in a short, narrow strip of wood that projects beyond the axle. (A little soap on the axles will make the wheels turn more easily.)

A Cannon that Shoots

You can make your book-end cannon into a shooting cannon by modifying the barrel and its mounting. This is how you do it:

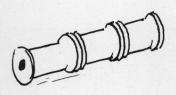

Make a new barrel using three thread spools glued together. (Scrape off the paper labels before you glue.) The holes down the center must line up perfectly when you glue the spools together.

When the glue has dried (in about a half hour), file and sandpaper the barrel to the shape you want.

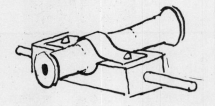

Make the mounting from a piece of 1-inch by 2-inch pine. File a large groove in the top, and drill two holes for dowels in the sides. Glue two short lengths of dowels into these holes, then attach the barrel to this mounting by means of a strip of copper or tin screwed down tightly.

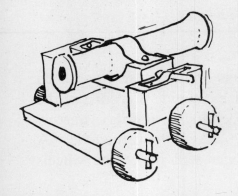

Now, attach the new barrel to the carriage in place of your old one. (Or make an entirely new carriage.)

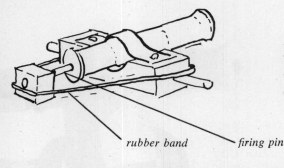

The firing pin is made from a 2½-inch length of ¼-inch dowel. Drill a ¼-inch hole in a small, square piece of wood and glue the dowel into this hole.

rubber band   *firing pin*

The cannon is fired by attaching a rubber band, as shown, and pulling back the firing pin. When a bullet (a short piece of dowel) is placed in the muzzle, and the firing pin is released—BANG—the bullet will be shot out. Practice your aim by trying to shoot bullets into a little cardboard box. Or, make a small upright cardboard target that will fall down each time you score a direct hit.

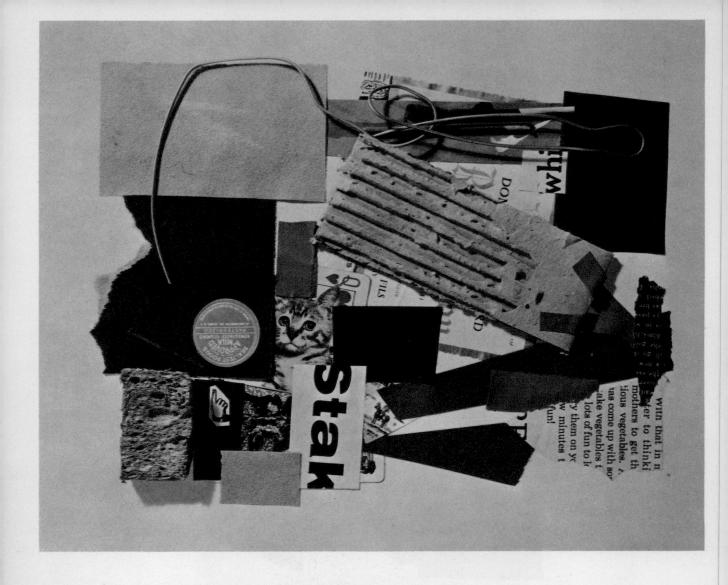

Odds-and-Ends Pictures – Collage

The pirate described on page 30 was made by combining thread spools. The giraffe pictured on page 34 was made by combining pieces of wood. Pictures, too, can be made by combining different materials. A picture made in this way is called a "collage," pronounced *coal-ahj.* This is a French word meaning "pasting," and the technique was first used by artists in France some fifty years ago.

To make a collage you need a pair of scissors, some paste, perhaps a needle and thread, a large sheet of paper for the background, and a willingness to rummage around collecting all sorts of bits and pieces and odds and ends and scraps.

There are three basic approaches to collage. The first is a *design* approach. The artist wants to construct a picture that is handsome because of its combination of colors and shapes and textures and materials. It is pleasant to look at a painting with two colors that go well together; it is just as pleasant to see a collage with a number of different elements that combine—or contrast—in an interesting fashion. The collage at the top of this page is interesting from a *design* point of view.

The second approach to collage involves selecting materials which are strange or provocative or surprising in combination. You can get some startling effects by cutting out and combining photographs and illustrations of things that do not ordinarily go together. For example, a picture of a big and ugly frog pasted on the forehead of a dignified old gentleman with whiskers would be quite shocking. A picture of a huge, clumsy elephant standing on top of the photograph of a delicate wineglass would have the same effect. A school of artists called *surrealists* painted pictures and made collages in a manner similar to this. Salvador Dali, with his fur-lined teacups, and melting pocket watches, is a member of this group.

The third approach to collage is *realistic*. The illustration above is of this sort. Realism can be both amusing and very attractive. Part of the humor may be due to the use of unlikely materials. For example, the gentleman illustrated above has a mustache made of steel wool, a nose that is a strip of red felt, and real feathers in his lapel.

There are no how-to-do-it instructions for this section on collage, because you can do so many different things. And what you do depends on what materials you can assemble. Almost anything is usable in a collage—pieces of plain or printed fabrics, leaves, twine, silver paper, corrugated cardboard, burlap, lace, copper screening, feathers, tacks, yarn, ribbons, sandpaper, old wallpaper and gift-wrapping paper, wood shavings, etc., etc. And newspapers and magazines contain a wide variety of photographs and drawings from which to select in making a surrealist collage. Collect all your odds and ends before you start to work. Then consider them for a while. They will often suggest ideas.

A collage can be made in three dimensions as well as on a flat surface. What do you call this sort of thing? Is it a collage, a construction, a sculpture, or a stage setting? Whatever you call it, the results can be quite exciting and very dramatic.

You will need more substantial materials for this kind of collage than those suitable for a flat, "pasted" collage. A piece of wood for a base is essential. And such materials as cardboard, corrugated board, wire, thread, thin dowels, thumbtacks, little blocks of wood, and paints will come in handy, in addition to the odds and ends used for a conventional collage.

Try for a variety of three-dimensional effects. You can create funny situations, or make the stage setting for a play or story. Or, how about a pleasing design of shapes and colors and textures? Make up your own rules —there is no tradition to follow. You are on your own!

*This three-dimensional collage uses corrugated
board, a chestnut, wood, sticks, paper,
and a feather, as well as a piece of garlic.*